USiNG PROBLEM SOLViNG
iN TEACHiNG AND TRAiNiNG

LEROY FORD

Illustrated by Joe McCormick
Based on author's original sketches

Multi-
Media
#5

BROADMAN PRESS * *Nashville, Tennessee*

© Copyright 1971 • Broadman Press
Nashville, Tennessee
All rights reserved
4234–15
ISBN: 0–8054–3415–1

Dewey Decimal Classification Number: 268.6
Library of Congress Catalog Card Number: 77–178060
Printed in the United States of America

Contents

The search for a way to express learning theory and techniques in an interesting, readable style led to the development of the cartooned-writing approach used in this and other books by the author. Most readers agree that they grasp and retain ideas better when the ideas receive exaggerated or absurd treatment through cartooning.

Most of the cartoons in this book found expression first as stick figures. Sometimes the stimulation of a class or conference session gave rise to an idea which the author later translated into stick-figure cartoons on the chalkboard. Sometimes ideas came from personal and family experiences. Significant statements in books sometimes suggested humorous nonverbal ways to express ideas.

"Cartooned writing" seeks to carry through pictures the weight of a message. Verbal symbols (words) added to the cartoons help clarify meaning and provide continuity of thought.

I wish to express appreciation to artist Joe McCormick for his assistance in sharpening the original cartoons. Karen Panovich kept the project moving and made helpful suggestions for improving the manuscript.

*Multi-Media Publications by LeRoy Ford

Number 1: *Primer for Teachers and Leaders*
Number 2: *Using the Lecture in Teaching and Training*
Number 3: *Using the Case Study in Teaching and Training*
Number 4: *Using the Panel in Teaching and Training*
Number 5: *Using Problem Solving in Teaching and Training*

Other Books by the Author

Tools for Teaching and Training
Developing Skills for Church Leaders

*Multi-Media publications are available in book, filmstrip, and chart set format.

4

A PROBLEM IS A PROBLEM!

This is a picture of all the people in the world who don't have problems!

Most people get in a mess now and then!

Sooner or later most everyone gets in a s-q-u-e-e-z-e!

We face intellectual problems.

We face decisions in matters of ethics.

We face spiritual problems.

But we learn when we face problems and seek to solve them—alone or with others.

"IT IS GOOD FOR ME THAT I HAVE BEEN AFFLICTED; THAT I MIGHT LEARN THY STATUTES."

(PSALM 119: 71)

Some problems . . .

Problems differ from objectives.

In a real sense, learning means overcoming problems of one kind or another.

We reach objectives by overcoming problems.

Problem solving and learning have much in common.

SOME EDUCATORS EQUATE PROBLEM
SOLVING WITH THINKING AND LEARNING.

THIS BOOK DEALS WITH THE USE OF THE PROBLEM SOLVING APPROACH IN GROUP DISCUSSION. WE WILL CALL IT...

GROUP PROBLEM SOLVING

OR

FORMAL DISCUSSION

LET'S DEFINE

GROUP PROBLEM SOLVING

(FORMAL DISCUSSION)

Group problem solving is . . .

- A LEARNING METHOD IN WHICH
- A GROUP
- USES A SYSTEMATIC DISCUSSION APPROACH IN WHICH THEY
- DEFINE THE PROBLEM,
- GET THE FACTS,
- FIT THE FACTS TOGETHER,
- DETERMINE POSSIBLE SOLUTIONS, AND
- CHOOSE THE BEST SOLUTIONS

A *problem* is . . .

...AN APPLE HIGHER THAN
YOU CAN REACH...

...A MOUNTAIN YOU CAN'T CLIMB!

. . . or a truth you can't quite comprehend.

A *problem* is a state of disorder!

Some people try to solve problems this way!

In group problem solving, we take these steps in a discussion:

Step 1 . . .

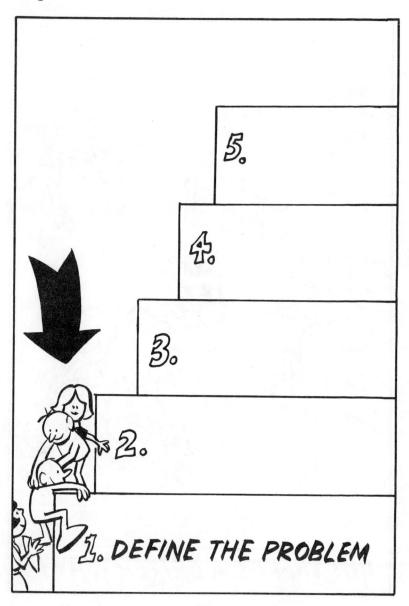

5.

4.

3.

2.

1. DEFINE THE PROBLEM

Step 3 . . .

5.

4.

3. **FIT THE FACTS TOGETHER**

2. **GET THE FACTS**

1. **DEFINE THE PROBLEM**

5.

4. DETERMINE POSSIBLE SOLUTIONS

3. FIT THE FACTS TOGETHER

2. GET THE FACTS

1. DEFINE THE PROBLEM

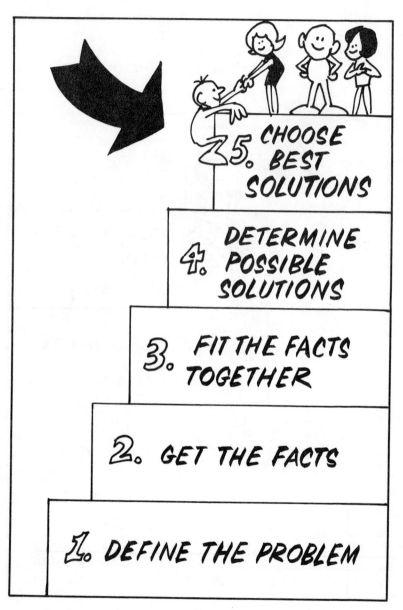

We may or may not take the steps in sequence!

DEFINE THE PROBLEM

CHOOSE BEST
SOLUTIONS

GET THE
FACTS

DETERMINE
POSSIBLE
SOLUTIONS

FIT THE FACTS
TOGETHER

WHEN THIS FELLOW BEGAN TO "FIT THE
FACTS TOGETHER" HE DECIDED TO
RE-DEFINE THE PROBLEM.

Now, just for fun, complete this definition . . .

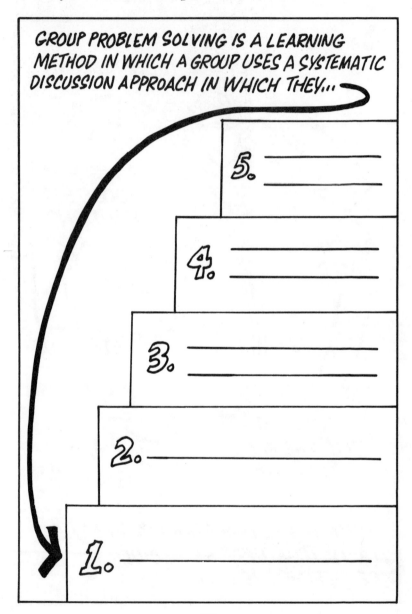

GROUP PROBLEM SOLVING IS A LEARNING METHOD IN WHICH A GROUP USES A SYSTEMATIC DISCUSSION APPROACH IN WHICH THEY...

5. _____

4. _____

3. _____

2. _____

1. _____

GROUP PROBLEM SOLVING SERVES MANY PURPOSES

Teachers and leaders use group problem solving to . . .

1. Expose the broad scope of a problem.

2. Develop skill in inductive thinking.

3. Encourage creativity.

4. Encourage group sharing of ideas.

5. Discourage "jumping at conclusions."

6. Help learners view problems objectively.

1. Problem solving groups use the approach to expose the broad scope of a problem.

WE HAVE TO GET "BELOW THE SURFACE" TO SOLVE SOME PROBLEMS.

For example,
    This problem . . .

. . . may become this problem.

2. Teachers and leaders use group problem solving to develop skill in inductive thinking.

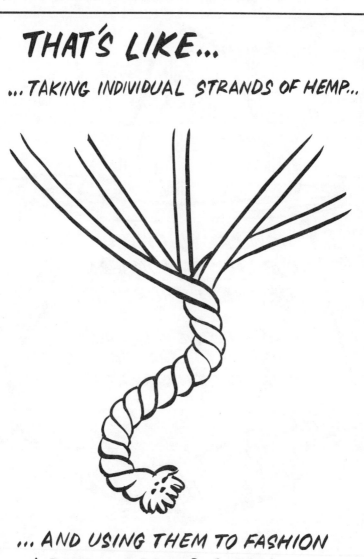

In inductive thinking we use examples, facts, and evidence to arrive at reliable principles or solutions.

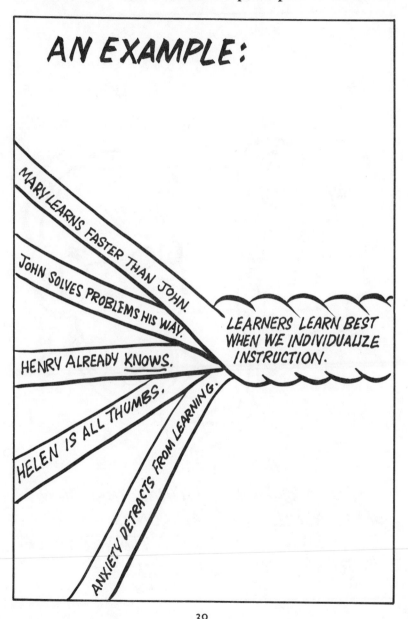

AN EXAMPLE:

MARY LEARNS FASTER THAN JOHN.

JOHN SOLVES PROBLEMS HIS WAY.

HENRY ALREADY KNOWS.

HELEN IS ALL THUMBS.

ANXIETY DETRACTS FROM LEARNING.

LEARNERS LEARN BEST WHEN WE INDIVIDUALIZE INSTRUCTION.

3. We use formal discussion to encourage creativity.

Creativity means using materials that are known . . .

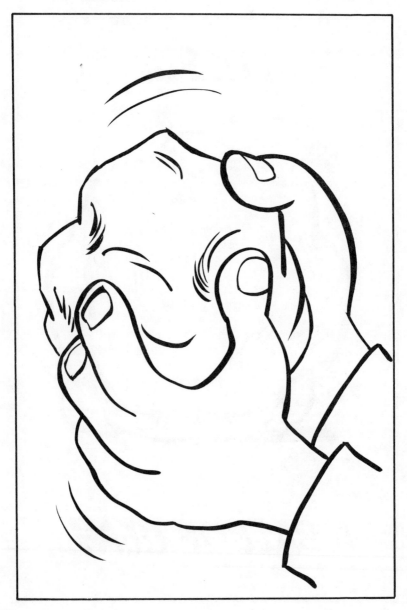

. . . a unique . . .

. . . **product.**

In group problem solving, this means . . .

... USING THE FACTS

AND RESOURCES THAT

ARE KNOWN...

TO PRODUCE

NEW, WORKABLE, AND

SATISFYING ANSWERS.

4. We use group problem solving to encourage group sharing.

> " LET EACH ONE
> SERVE THE GROUP
> TO THE MEASURE OF
> HIS ENDOWMENT. "
>
> (I PETER 4:10,
> BERKELEY)

5. We use group problem solving to discourage "jumping to conclusions!"

6. We can use group problem solving to lead learners to view problems objectively.

Now, write the purpose of group problem solving which each of these "word cues" suggests:

1. ICEBERG: _____

_____

_____

2. ROPE: _____

_____

_____

3. CLAY: _____

_____

_____

4. BIBLE: _____

_____

_____

5. SWIMMING: _____

_____

_____

6. CHAIRS: _____

_____

_____

LET'S LOOK AT

STEP ONE:

DEFINE THE PROBLEM

Problem solving groups find these guidelines helpful in defining problems:

1. *Write* the problem down!

2. State a *trial* problem first.

3. State the problem as a *question*.

4. Test the question for *double* meaning.

5. Test the question for *impartial* wording.

6. Make the question "reasonably" *specific*.

7. Use questions of *fact, policy, value,* or *speculation*.

8. Decide which *level* of the problem to attack.

9. Attack the *right* problem!

1. *Write* it down! Sometimes the biggest job is picking up the pencil!

2. You will probably state a "trial" problem first . . .

. . . **and polish it up later!**

3. State the problem as a *question* which calls for critical analysis and exploratory thinking. (Or as an assertion to be proved or disproved.)

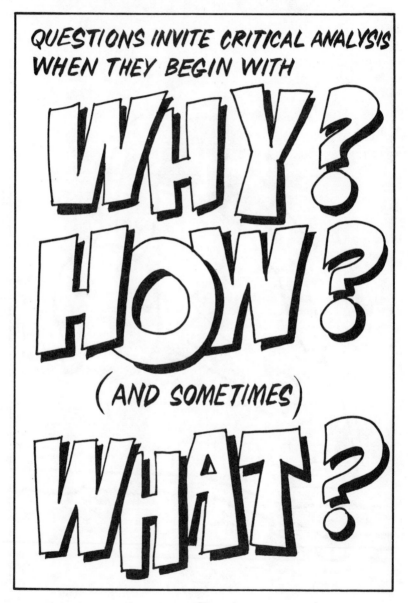

For example:

1. (WHAT) SHOULD BE THE RELATIONSHIP OF CHURCH, STATE, AND SCHOOL IN AMERICAN DEMOCRACY?

2. (HOW) CAN PARENTS AND TEACHERS WORK TOGETHER TO PROVIDE NON-PROFESSIONAL HELPERS FOR THE CLASSROOM?

3. (WHY) HAS STUDENT PARTICIPATION IN STUDENT COUNCIL ELECTIONS INCREASED THIS YEAR?

4. Test the question for *double* meaning—for ambiguous words?

SOME QUESTIONS, LIKE OPTICAL ILLUSIONS, PRESENT MORE THAN ONE PICTURE.

5. Test the question for impartial wording.

6. Make the question "reasonably" *specific.*

7. Use questions of *"fact," "policy," "value,"* and *"speculation."*

FOR EXAMPLE:

FACT: WHAT WAS THE SEQUENCE OF EVENTS LEADING TO JESUS' CRUCIFIXION?

VALUE: HOW SHOULD THE CHRISTIAN RESPOND TO THE "NEW MORALITY"?

POLICY: HOW CAN WE HALT THE EXODUS OF QUALIFIED TEACHERS FROM OUR STATE?

SPECULATION: HOW WILL THE CLERICAL WORKERS RESPOND TO THE NEW ORGANIZATION?

8. Decide which *level* of the problem to attack.
   For example, this problem has several levels . . .

WHO LEFT THE GARBAGE OUT, ANYWAY?

WHAT KIND OF POISON GETS 'EM QUICKEST?

HOW CAN "BIG CITY" IMPROVE GARBAGE COLLECTION?

HOW CAN "BIG CITY" KEEP ITS STREETS AND ALLEYS CLEAN?

HOW CAN "BIG CITY" CREATE A HEALTHFUL ENVIRONMENT FOR ITS CITIZENS?

Many problems are like FLEAS!

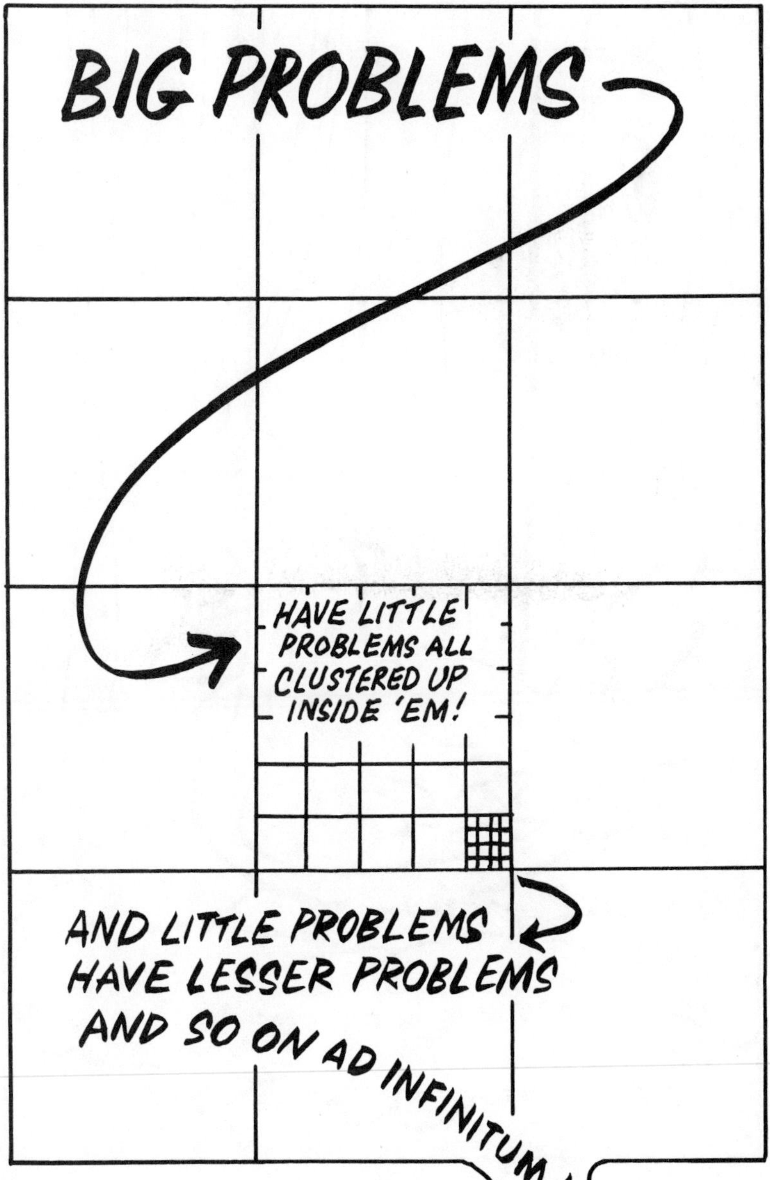

BIG PROBLEMS

HAVE LITTLE
PROBLEMS ALL
CLUSTERED UP
INSIDE 'EM!

AND LITTLE PROBLEMS
HAVE LESSER PROBLEMS
AND SO ON AD INFINITUM!

9. Attack the *right* problem! Some people concentrate on a problem . . .

. . . and work it through to a solution, only to discover that they have been . . .

. . . sitting on the wrong nest!

Remember . . .

"*A PROBLEM*

WELL-DEFINED

IS

HALF-SOLVED"

... JOHN DEWEY

Now, look at these "word cues" and write the guidelines for defining problems:

1. WRITE: _____
_____

2. TRIAL: _____
_____

3. QUESTION: _____
_____

4. DOUBLE: _____
_____

5. IMPARTIAL: _____
_____

6. SPECIFIC: _____
_____

7. FACT: _____
_____

8. LEVEL: _____
_____

9. RIGHT: _____
_____

LET'S LOOK AT
STEP TWO:

GET THE FACTS

Problem solving groups follow the guidelines in getting the facts:

1. Write a narrative of the situation.

2. Get the whole story. Ask, What's missing?

3. Talk to persons concerned or with a subject matter expert.

4. Check the records.

5. Get opinions and feelings.

6. Consider factors of limitation.

7. Let the facts help you state—or restate the problem.

1. Write a narrative of the situation.

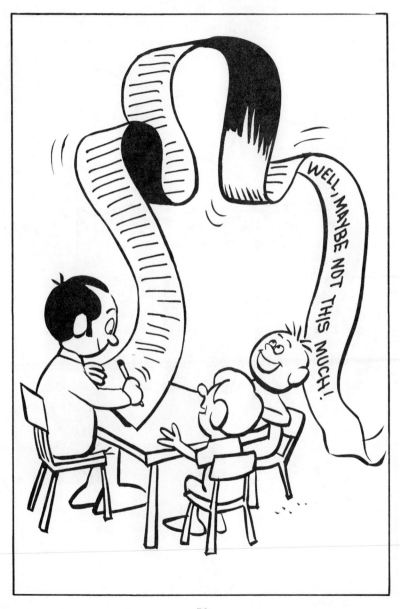

2. Get the whole story. Ask: What's missing? Do we have the whole story?

Like a kaleidoscope, the more pieces (*facts*) we have in the drum, the more possible patterns (*answers*).

3. Talk with persons concerned—or with the . . .

...SUBJECT MATTER EXPERT!

4. Check the records. They have a lot to say!

5. Get opinions and feelings.

6. Consider the factors of limitation. We have to work with them, too.

CONSIDER THINGS YOU COULDN'T CHANGE IF YOU WANTED TO... POLICIES FOR EXAMPLE.

7. Let the facts help you state—or restate—the problem!

"AND YOU SAID HE HAD AN ULCER!"

"WE CAN HAVE FACTS
WITHOUT THINKING BUT
WE CANNOT HAVE
THINKING WITHOUT FACTS."

...JOHN DEWEY

Now, look at these "picture cues" and write the guidelines for getting the facts.

...SUBJECT MATTER EXPERT!

"AND YOU SAID HE HAD AN ULCER!"

LET'S LOOK AT

STEP THREE:

FIT THE FACTS TOGETHER

Teachers and leaders find these guidelines helpful in analyzing the facts!

1. Organize facts into groups of related facts.

2. Get familiar with the facts.

3. Isolate the facts out of which the problem grows.

4. Determine which facts have a bearing on other facts.

5. Keep asking, *Why* is this a fact? Learn to probe!

1. Organize facts into groups of related facts.

GROUP 1:

GROUP 2:

GROUP 3:

GROUP 4

2. Get familiar with the facts—make friends of them. Have them at your fingertips.

You must have facts to solve problems. Try this problem . . .

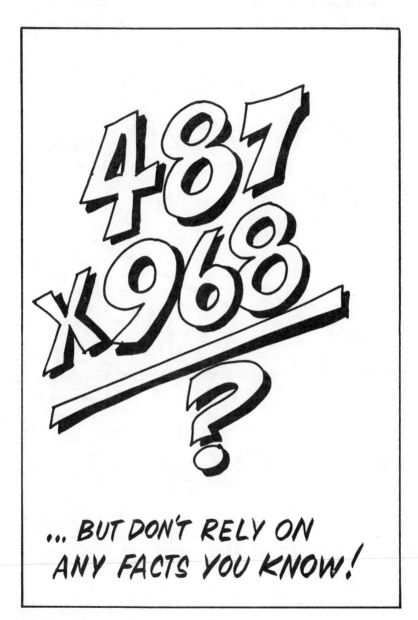

Problem solving on higher levels requires ability to reach back at will . . .

. . . and pull forward the knowledge or facts to use as problem solving tools.

3. Isolate the facts out of which the problem grows.

FOR EXAMPLE:

ENROLLMENT 121

ATTENDANCE 4

VISITS THIS WEEK 0

4. Determine which facts have a bearing on other facts.

Some solutions come through sudden insight—through what some folks call the . . .

... **AH-HA!** moment!

And now, look at these "picture cues" and write the guideline each suggests.

GROUP 1:
GROUP 2:
GROUP 3:
GROUP 4

_____

_____

_____

_____

FOR EXAMPLE:

ENROLLMENT 121
ATTENDANCE 4
VISITS THIS WEEK 0

_____

_____

ENROLLMENT 121
ATTENDANCE 4
VISITS THIS WEEK 0

AH-HA!

_____

_____

WHY?

... IS THIS A FACT?

_____

_____

LET'S LOOK AT
STEP FOUR:

DETERMINE POSSIBLE SOLUTIONS

Problem solving groups find these guidelines helpful in determining possible solutions:

1. Free your imagination! Think of new and *creative* solutions!

2. Provide time for *incubation* of ideas. Everybody has the right to wonder!

3. Consider all *sides* of the problem.

4. Brainstorm possible solutions. Get ideas in *rapid-fire* order.

5. Learn to *defer* judgment.

6. Apply the technique of *"forced relationships."*

7. Ask small *study* groups to suggest solutions.

1. **Free your imagination! Think of new and creative solutions!**

2. Provide time for incubation of ideas. Everybody has the right to wonder!

LEARN TO WAIT THAT THIRTY-SECOND ETERNITY WHILE GROUP MEMBERS THINK IN SILENCE!

3. Consider all sides of the problem . . .

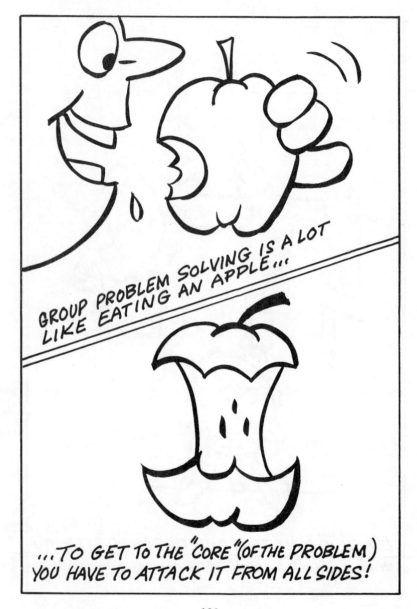

4. Brainstorm possible solutions. Get ideas in rapid-fire order!

5. **Learn to defer judgment.** "Deferred judgment" in the brainstorming method encourages free flow of ideas.

6. Apply the technique of "forced" relationships. For example . . .

PROBLEM: IN WHAT WAYS CAN WE DISPLAY THIS POSTER TO PUBLICIZE ACTEENS?

	We Can staple it.	We Can bend it.	We Can burn it.	We Can Cut it.	It's semi-rigid
ACTEENS MEET TUESDAY 8:00 P.M. FACTS					
We Can Staple it.					
We Can bend it.					
We Can burn it.					
We Can Cut it.					
It's semi-rigid.					
It's Printed on one Side.					

WE KNOW TWO FACTS: (1) WE CAN BEND THE
CARDBOARD; (2) WE CAN STAPLE IT. BECAUSE
WE KNOW THESE TWO FACTS, WE CAN THINK
OF SUCH POSSIBLE SOLUTIONS AS THESE.

When we use the technique of forced relationships with the primary colors . . .

	RED ⬇	BLUE ⬇	YELLOW ⬇
RED ➡	RED	*Purple*	*Orange*
BLUE ➡	*Purple*	BLUE	*Green*
YELLOW ➡	*Orange*	*Green*	YELLOW

. . . WE GET THREE *New* **COLORS!**

7. Ask small study groups to suggest solutions—based on facts.

" EACH GROUP SUGGEST SIX POSSIBLE SOLUTIONS "

To review, look at these "word cues" and write the guideline each suggests for determining solutions.

1. CREATIVE: _____
_____
_____

2. INCUBATION: _____
_____
_____

3. APPLE: _____
_____
_____

4. RAPID-FIRE: _____
_____
_____

5. DEFER: _____

_____

_____

6 FORCED: _____

_____

_____

7. STUDY GROUPS: _____

_____

_____

LET'S LOOK AT
STEP FIVE:

CHOOSE THE BEST SOLUTIONS

Problem solving groups find these guidelines helpful in choosing best solution(s).

1. Determine criteria for acceptable solutions.

2. Adopt a rating system to determine how well the solution meets the criteria.

3. Evaluate each possible solution in light of criteria *and* the rating system.

4. Use a guidesheet to insure adequate attention to each step.

1. Determine criteria for acceptable solutions.

FOR EXAMPLE:

1. HOW WILL IT AFFECT _YOU_?

2. HOW WILL IT AFFECT OTHERS?

3. HOW WILL IT AFFECT THE ORGANIZATION?

2. Adopt a rating system to determine how well the solution meets the criteria.

FOR EXAMPLE:

SYMBOL

	YES! NO DOUBT ABOUT IT!
	DOUBTFUL. MAY OR MAY NOT WORK.
	NO. AVOID AT ALL COSTS!

3. Evaluate each possible solution in the light of the criteria *and* the rating system.

FOR EXAMPLE:

THE PROBLEM:

LITTLE BO PEEP
   HAS LOST HER SHEEP
AND CAN'T TELL WHERE
   TO FIND HIM!

IT'S BEEN THREE DAYS
   SINCE HE WENT OUT
      TO GRAZE
AND NONE OF THE NEIGHBORS
   HAS SPIED HIM!

POSSIBLE SOLUTIONS

CRITERIA →	HOW WILL IT AFFECT BO PEEP?	HOW WILL IT AFFECT THE SHEEP?	RATING SYSTEM ✓ YES! NO DOUBT ABOUT IT! ? DOUBTFUL. MAY OR MAY NOT WORK. ✗ NO. AVOID AT ALL COSTS!
	?	✗	1. SEE IF HOMEOWNER'S INSURANCE COVERS THE LOSS.
	✓	✓	2. CONTACT "MISSING SHEEP" BUREAU.
	*✓	*✓	3. LEAVE HIM ALONE AND HE'LL COME HOME WAGGING HIS TAIL BEHIND HIM!
	?	✗	4. BUY ANOTHER LAMB!
	✗	✗	5. REPAIR THE FENCE.
	✓	✓	6. COMB THE COUNTRYSIDE WITH A HUMAN CHAIN!

Use this guidesheet for . . .

I. DEFINE THE PROBLEM (Limit the field.)

Trial Statement of Problem

_____

_____

II. GET THE FACTS
(Be sure you have the whole story.)

Review the record
What are the factors of
   limitation?
Talk with persons concerned

Get opinions and feelings
What factors caused the
   problem to develop?

1. _____
2. _____
3. _____
4. _____
5. _____
6. _____
7. _____
8. _____
9. _____
10. _____

. . . formal discussion or problem solving.

Final Statement of Problem

_____

_____

III. FIT THE FACTS TOGETHER
Organize facts
Get familiar with them
Isolate most significant facts
Determine which facts have bearing on other facts
Probe—ask WHY?

IV. DETERMINE POSSIBLE SOLUTION(S)
1. _____
2. _____
3. _____
4. _____

V. CHOOSE BEST SOLUTION(S)   (√) Yes
(?) Questionable
(X) No

Possible actions:
1   2   3   4
☐ ☐ ☐ ☐   1. _____
_____

☐ ☐ ☐ ☐   2. _____
_____

☐ ☐ ☐ ☐   3. _____
_____

* Others have specified the steps this way . . .

I. Alex F. Osborn, *Applied Imagination:*
   1. Fact-finding
   2. Idea-finding
   3. Solution-finding

II. Sidney J. Parnes, *Creative Behavior Guidebook:*
   1. Fact-finding
   2. Problem-finding
   3. Idea-finding
   4. Solution-finding
   5. Acceptance-finding—Applying the Total Process

III. John W. Keltner, *Group Discussion Processes:*
   1. Formulate a problem
   2. Analyze the problem
   3. Set up standards for solution
   4. Find solutions for the problem
   5. Put your solution into action

IV. Thomas F. Staton, *How to Instruct Successfully:*
   1. Identify the problem
   2. Gather data
   3. Analyze the data
   4. Formulate hypotheses
   5. Test the hypotheses
   6. Formulate a conclusion or solution

V. John Dewey, *How We Think:*
   1. A difficulty (problem) is experienced.
   2. It is located and defined.
   3. Possible solutions are suggested.
   4. These possible solutions are examined and compared.
   5. Further observation and experiment lead to acceptance or rejection of each.
   6. The solution regarded as most tenable is subjected to further verification.

* See bibliography, page 125

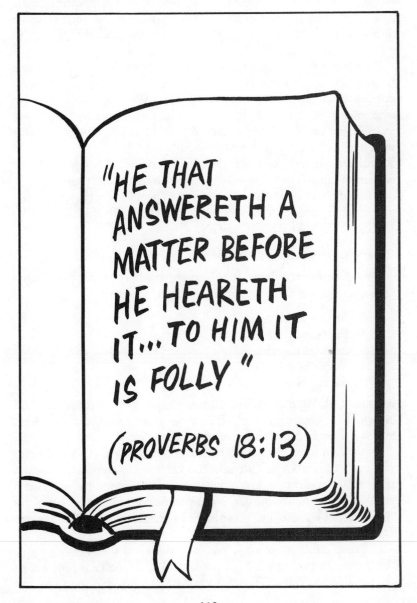

Book Summary

A problem is a problem! Most people get in a mess now and then. Sooner or later most every body gets into a s-q-u-e-e-z-e! People face intellectual problems, ethical problems, spiritual problems. But all of us learn when we face problems and seek to solve them—alone or with others. Some problems are not as big as others—but we can learn from all of them.

Problems differ from objectives. A problem is what keeps one from reaching an objective. In a real sense, learning means overcoming problems of one kind or another. We reach objectives by overcoming problems. A teacher becomes an effective teacher by overcoming problems such as lack of empathy, lack of skill in using methods, and lack of information.

Problem solving and learning have much in common. Some educators equate problem solving with thinking and learning.

This book deals with the use of the problem-solving approach in group discussion. We will call it GROUP PROBLEM SOLVING or FORMAL DISCUSSION.

Let's define group problem solving.

Group problem solving is a learning method in which a group uses a systematic discussion approach in which they

    define the problem
    get the facts
    fit the facts together
    determine possible solutions
    choose the best solutions.

Raymond M. Rigdon defines it more simply as "a learning method in which a group, through following several well-defined steps, explores a pertinent problem of mutual interest."

A problem is an apple higher than you can reach. It's a mountain you can't climb! Or it's a truth you can't quite comprehend—such as "But I say unto you, love your enemies." Someone has said that a problem is a state of disorder. Some people try to solve problems by "jumping on a horse and going off in four directions." But we can find better ways!

In group problem solving, we follow several well-defined steps. We define the problem and get the facts. We fit the facts together to get possible solutions. Then we evaluate the possible solutions and choose the better ones. We may or may not take the steps in sequence. When we fit the facts together, we may decide we need to redefine the problem.

Group problem solving serves many purposes.

1. Problem-solving groups use the approach to expose the broad scope of a problem. Problems, like iceburgs, have more "below" the surface than meets the eye. For example the problem "How to make an effective visit for the church" may become this problem: "How can we overcome *lack of concern* for the unchurched?"

2. Teachers and leaders use group problem solving to develop skill in inductive thinking. It's like taking individual strands of hemp and using them to fashion a rope. From facts and examples, learners arrive at principles.

3. We use problem solving to encourage creativity. A student had the wrong idea when she said, "Well, Miss Jones, I think that deep inside every person is a spark of creativity . . . and the teacher's role is to *water* that spark!" Creativity means taking materials that are known—like a ball of clay—and using them to fashion a unique product—like a one-of-a-kind vase. In group problem solving this means using facts and resources that are known—to produce new, workable, and satisfying answers.

4. We use group problem solving to encourage group sharing. Peter said, "Let each one serve the group to the measure of his endowment" (1 Pet. 4:10, Berkeley).

5. We use problem solving to discourage jumping at conclusions.

6. We can use group problem solving to lead learners to view problems objectively. A tradition-bound person might say, "We'll put the chairs in three rows of eight each." The objective person might say, "Who says we need chairs, anyway!"

Let's look at step one: DEFINE THE PROBLEM

Group problem solvers follow guidelines like these in defining the problem:

1. Write it down! Sometimes the biggest job is picking up the pencil. Writing forces precise communication.

2. State a trial problem first—and polish it up later. You may even discover you've worked on the wrong problem!

3. State the problem as a question which calls for critical analysis and exploratory thinking. For example: What should be the relationship of church, state, and school in American democracy?

4. Test the question for double meaning and for ambiguous words. We can illustrate "double meaning" with the statement a procedure writer used. She said, "Order a picture of Jesus ascending into heaven from the Baptist Book Store."

5. Test the question for impartial wording. One leader presented this problem: "What can we do to get teachers to quit using the outdated lecture method in teaching?"

6. Make the question reasonably specific. Discussion of very general problems leads to waste of time on meandering minutia.

7. Use questions of fact, policy, value, or speculation. For example, a fact question might look like this: What was the sequence of events leading to Jesus' crucifixion? A policy question might look like this: How can we halt the exodus of qualified teachers from our state? We might use this question as an example of a value question: How should the Christian respond to the "new morality"?

8. Decide which level of the problem to attack—the general, the specific, or the "in-between." Many problems are like fleas. "Big fleas have little fleas upon their backs to bite 'em. Little fleas have lesser fleas, and so on ad infinitum." Big problems have little problems all clustered up inside 'em. Little problems have lesser problems and so on ad infinitum!

9. Attack the right problem. Some groups concentrate on a problem, work it through to solution, only to discover they have been sitting on the wrong nest! John Dewey said, "A problem well defined is half solved."

Let's look at step two: GET THE FACTS

Group problem solvers find these guidelines helpful:

1. Write a narrative of the situation. Make it not too long; not too short.

2. Get the whole story. Keep asking, What's missing? Do we have the *whole* story?

3. Talk to subject matter experts. Sometimes we call them the SME.

4. Check the records. They may have a lot to say!

5. Get opinions and feelings. Persons may not base feelings on fact; but it's a fact that they do have feelings.

6. Consider factors of limitations—those facts of policy, for example, which one cannot change.

7. Let the facts help in restating the problem. New facts shed

new light. "We can have facts without thinking, but we cannot have thinking without facts," said John Dewey.

Let's look at step three: FIT THE FACTS TOGETHER

Group problem solvers find these guidelines helpful:

1. Organize facts into groups of related facts.
2. Get familiar with the facts. Make friends with them. One must have facts to solve problems. Problem solving on higher levels requires ability to reach back at will and pull forward the knowledge or facts to use as problem solving tools.
3. Isolate the facts out of which the problem grows. Some facts have little significance; others provide significant clues.
4. Determine which facts have a bearing on other facts. When enrolment has reached 121, but attendance has slipped to 4, we see why when we see that visits amounted to 0! Zero visits has a bearing on low attendance. Some solutions come through sudden insight—through what some folks call the AH-HA! moment. Insight usually results when facts take on a meaningful pattern.
5. Learn to probe. Keep asking WHY is this a fact? New facts become evident. Possible solutions begin to appear.

Let's look at step four: DETERMINE POSSIBLE SOLUTIONS.

These guidelines, applied, lead to possible solutions:

1. Free your imagination! Think of new and creative solutions. An absurd idea may generate some not-so-absurd ones.
2. Provide times for incubation of ideas. Everybody has the right to wonder! Learn to wait that thirty-second eternity while group members think in silence.
3. Consider all sides of the problem. Group problem solving is a lot like eating an apple—to get to the core you have to attack it from all sides!
4. Brainstorm possible solutions. Get ideas in rapid-fire order.
5. Learn to defer judgment. Deferred judgment in the brainstorming method encourages free flow of ideas.
6. Apply the technique of "forced" relationships among ideas and facts. For example, if one mixes in various ways the three primary colors, he creates three new colors. Playing one fact against several other facts leads to new and unique solutions.
7. Ask small study groups to suggest solutions.

Let's look at step five: CHOOSE THE BEST SOLUTIONS

Group problem solvers find these guidelines helpful in taking the last of the five steps:

1. Determine criteria for acceptable solutions. Different problems may require different criteria or standards. Criteria for problems dealing with interpersonal relationships might appear as follows: How will it affect YOU? How will it affect OTHERS? How will it affect the ORGANIZATION?

2. Adopt a rating system to determine how well the solution meets the criteria. Some problem solvers use this system:

✓ Yes!   ? Doubtful   X No!

3. Evaluate each possible solution in the light of criteria and the rating system. Test each solution. Select those which merit the highest number of positive values.

4. Use a guidesheet for group problem solving to insure attention to all steps.

Problem solving in groups provides a thorough and effective approach to study of many problems. It assures thorough analysis. It increases the probability of wise decisions. "He that answereth a matter before he heareth it, it is folly . . . unto him" (Prov. 18:13).

Bibliography

Dewey, John, *How We Think*. New York: D. C. Heath and Company, 1933.

Hudgins, Bryce B., *Problem Solving in the Classroom*. New York: The Macmillan Company, 1966.

Keltner, John W., *Group Discussion Practices*. New York: Longmans, Green, and Company, 1957.

Osborn, A., *Applied Imagination*. New York: Charles Scribner's Sons, 1963.

Parnes, Sidney J., *Creative Behavior Guidebook*. New York: Charles Scribner's Sons, 1967.

Potter, David, and Anderson, Martin P., *Discussion, a Guide to Effective Practice*. Belmont, California: Wadsworth Publishing Company, Inc. 1963.

Schmuck, Richard, and Chesler, Mark, and Lippitt, Ronald, *Problem Solving to Improve Classroom Learning*. Chicago: Science Research Associates, 1966.

Smith, William S., *Group Problem Solving Through Discussion*, New York: Bobbs-Merrill Company, Inc., 1965

Station, Thomas F., *How to Instruct Successfully*, New York: McGraw-Hill Book Company, Inc., 1960